London Buses 20

David Stewart

Capital Transport

ISBN 1 85414 268 2

Published by Capital Transport Publishing
38 Long Elmes, Harrow Weald, Middlesex

Printed by CS Graphics, Singapore

Contents

The front cover photograph is by Mark Lyons.

Title page The most numerous double-deck body type in London is the Alexander ALX400, built in long and short versions on the three main low-floor chassis available. A typical example seen at Hampton Court is London United's VA101, a 10.1m model on Volvo B7TL chassis, branded for route 111. *Mark Lyons*

Left Perhaps the standard double-decker of the 1990s in London was the Leyland (later the Volvo) Olympian with Northern Counties bodywork, and all the main operators in London took some. Although there are plenty still around, some are now being cascaded out of London, and the large groups are well placed to do this. NV73 in Blackfriars Road is from the batch that London Central and General have been busily sending up to Go-Ahead North East. *Colin Stannard*

Introduction

This book gives details as at January 2003 of buses that operate on London Bus services within the TfL (Transport for London) framework. We acknowledge the assistance given by some of the operating companies. Vehicle information is extracted principally from the records of the London Omnibus Traction Society (LOTS) and readers needing regular updated information are recommended to membership of LOTS or the PSV Circle. Fleet lists can be found in other specialist fleet publications from LOTS and British Bus Publishing. In this book, each main vehicle type is reviewed in order of chassis make, coupled with a selection of pictures. Where route numbers are quoted, readers are referred to the bus maps readily available in London.

On 1st April 2000, London Transport Buses (LTB) became London Bus Services Ltd (LBSL), trading publicly as 'London Buses' (LB), and falling within the remit of Transport for London (TfL) which became fully operational from 3rd July 2000, following the election of Ken Livingstone as Mayor in May 2000. London Buses controls the bus service network in Greater London, and offers and awards route tenders. Every bus route in London operates either under a direct contract or within an operating agreement with London Buses. In recent times, several of the commercial routes running within Greater London under operating agreements have come under full LB auspices, including routes 216, 354, 358 and 418 during 2002. Part of the Mayor's strategy is to improve bus service quality and, since 28th April 2001, most new route contracts in London have been let on a 'Quality' basis, with stricter requirements for reliability, and which can incur penalty payments for poor performance.

By summer 2001, passenger levels began to rise at an increasing rate, and this has been sustained. While traffic congestion and parking difficulties played their part, action on fares was also important. Bus fares were generally capped, there was improved validity and new categories of certain Travelcards and all-day Bus Passes, and new Saver Tickets – which gave discounts – were introduced. In 2003, London bus fares still remain relatively low by national standards, and trials of smart-cards were ongoing at the beginning of the year, whilst it was TfL's intention to promote the idea of 'cash-less' buses as far as possible. A long-term trial on route W7 remains ongoing, and articulated buses already in operation on Red Arrow routes 507 and 521, together with those introduced early in 2003 on routes 436 and 453, work on this basis. Passengers all have to have pre-paid tickets or passes before boarding.

It soon became evident that some single-deck routes needed more capacity and were gradually converted to double-deck. Routes 79, 105, 106, 156, 183, 191, 204, 257, 258, 307, 344, 345, C2, and E3 are examples that have been so treated in 2001/2, and several more routes (including 20, 34, 139, 189, 217, 231, 282 and 321) are in the pipeline for the first half of 2003. Not only that, but an increasing trend throughout 2002 has been frequency increases on route after route, often coupled with better evening and Sunday services.

Furthermore, the Mayor's Congestion Charging Area in central London prompted many changes to bus routes, to allow for a predicted increase of 7000 passengers per day in and around the area. Three totally new routes (148, 205 and 414) were introduced in autumn 2002. These provide extra capacity over existing corridors, whilst also giving new direct travel opportunities. Over the winter/spring of 2002/3, other routes are being split, for example the 10, 36, 53, 63 and 133 into 10/390, 36/436, 53/453, 63/363 and 133/333, effectively shortening each segment into overlapping sections and giving more buses overall. The result of all these actions is a substantial increase in the overall bus fleet in London, for the first time in around forty years. Over 400 extra buses were needed to service the pvr (peak vehicle requirement) between the beginning and the end of 2002, and around another 400 extra buses will be needed to cover higher pvrs in the first half of 2003.

This huge increase in the London bus fleet is good news for passengers and enthusiasts, but it is not without problems and adverse consequences. It has cost a prodigious amount of money and, towards the end of 2002 TfL was predicting a heavy shortfall of finance for 2003. A feature of recent times is that in almost every case of a contract route renewal, London Buses has called for new buses, with a view to renewing virtually the whole London fleet in a fairly short time-span. Around 1300 new buses were delivered during 2002, with about a third simply to provide for the pvr increase. Double-decking of several routes has meant that replacement of around 400 single-deck buses during 2001/2/3 led to potential orders for the likes of the Dart being converted into orders for Tridents and Volvo B7TLs. About 150 of these double-deck buses were for First London, who had been Marshall's main customer for several years for bodywork on its Darts. Perhaps the reduction in orders had some bearing on the close-down of the Cambridge bodybuilder in August 2002.

Manufacturers were under pressure to deliver so many new buses, and some type conversions had to be delayed or covered by older buses for varying periods of time, and this process is ongoing. The extra pvr has produced a severe pressure on garage space, and the sell-off of redundant garages in the 1990s has proved – with hindsight – to be an unfortunate decision.

Docklands Buses had been around for a number of years, latterly on private contract services. When they won their first London Buses contract in March 2002, they became the only new entrant into London work during the year. The Caetano Nimbus body started to gain London orders in 2001/2, all from smaller operators, but cessation of production of rival bodies on the Dart by Alexander and Marshall during 2002 saw Caetano's fortunes improved by the awarding of new orders from First London. HV02 OZX is a 10.5m Nimbus on the 10-metre Dart SLF chassis, pausing at Gants Hill on route 167. *Gerald Mead*

TfL has tried to seek new sites for bus garages in London, with space being leased to potential operators. Already, TfL own existing garages such as Ash Grove and Edgware, each of which is used by two operators. Initial successes included the acquisition of the old Brixton Hill tram depot, which was to be used from spring 2003 by Arriva as an outstation from the nearby Brixton Garage, and of a former parcels depot at Perivale which was to be used by Thorpe's. At the turn of 2002/3 moves were afoot from TfL to restore the old Walworth Garage to operational status. Stagecoach acquired more land alongside Stratford Garage and demolished buildings at Catford to get more parking space. First obtained a larger base at Rainham, more space alongside Westbourne Park Garage and in the council depot at Greenford. Metroline obtained a former lorry firm's base at Perivale and Arriva re-opened Stamford Hill and got a little more land by Edmonton Garage.

The portfolio of London operators reduced in 2002, with three departures and one arrival. The arrival was Docklands Buses, who won route 167 in March. First to go was Durham Travel Services (London Easylink) who closed down without warning on 21st August, leaving its two routes (42 and 185) to be farmed out to various operators until a more permanent solution could be found. DTS's buses were removed by the Receiver and put up for sale. From 1st November all of the Metropolitan Omnibus routes and buses were transferred to Thorpe's in an amicable settlement, and Thorpe's incorporated them into their own operation. Two days later, Sovereign Buses London was sold to the Transdev group, and was put under the management of London United. The DTS close-down and the Sovereign sale were partly attributed to losses incurred by penalty payments to London Buses due to poor performance. In turn, the poor performance was mainly due to driver shortages. By late 2002, the large pvr increase referred to above was presenting increasing problems in driver recruitment and retention, already a difficult area to manage.

London Buses' 80%-red livery rule for the central Zone 1 is now universal, and has spread inexorably, under pressure from TfL, to the outer reaches of the Capital. Operators on the periphery such as Crystals, Epsom Buses and Wing's Buses adopted all-over red, although there was not really a need to do so. Mitcham Belle, Armchair and Tellings-Golden Miller were coerced to adopt a mainly red colour scheme for new buses delivered in 2002, but each managed to incorporate their house colours somewhere on the livery. Corporate identities of the major groups continue to be evident, although all have adapted their national styles to the standards of London Buses, while there are still small pockets of vehicles in older company liveries, in the suburban outskirts.

Vehicle developments during 2002 were steady rather than revolutionary, and most new vehicle deliveries were more of the same. However, small numbers of the Mercedes-Benz Citaro came to First London (in standard single-deck form) and to London General (in articulated mode), and more of the latter arrived over the turn of 2002/3 for new routes 436 and 453. The first examples of Scania's new OmniCity single-decker and OmniDekka double-decker were arriving with Metrobus. Large numbers of step-entrance buses, and even a few early model low-floor buses, were sold off or cascaded within the large groups to their provincial operations. TransBus International, owners of Dennis, Plaxton and Alexander, made further moves towards a corporate image, although the established models continued to be produced. Already the edges were blurred, with transfer in 2001 of production of the Plaxton Pointer body to Alexander's Falkirk factory. The Plaxton President is produced at the former Northern Counties facility at Wigan, and the ALX400 double-decker at either Falkirk or at Alexander's other plant in Belfast. However, a new TransBus range of single- and double-deck designs grouped under the 'Enviro' name began to make itself known, and examples will undoubtedly appear in London.

Routemasters

In a world where new low-floor buses are arriving in quantity, the survival of the aged Routemaster is more and more of an anachronism. Nevertheless, it is an icon of London. On tourist posters and publicity, on mugs and postcards, it is up there with Beefeaters, Bobbies, Big Ben and Tower Bridge. After the rush to get rid of them in the 1980s and early 1990s, those that were left began to gain cult status. Politically, it became difficult to contemplate converting their last few routes to modern buses. In the mid-1990s most received refurbishments with new engines and gearboxes and a modernised interior treatment. By 2001 TfL had bought a number back from other operators and private owners, and these went through a refurbishment programme to return to service. A few more were sourced during 2002. Even with around 650 in stock, pvr increases on some of their routes have meant that there are still not enough to go round. Inevitably, one or two of the twenty Routemaster routes will have to be converted to allow others to be fully stocked. Furthermore, requirements for full accessibility to all passengers will eventually cause mainstream Routemaster routes to be reduced to those where an alternative accessible service is available. They will be around for a few years yet, but in time will be limited to 'heritage' status.

Facing page There are still well over 600 Routemasters serving central London, on twenty routes. The longer RML is a 30-foot long 72-seater and is the mainstay on most of the routes. All but one or two have been refurbished and re-engined over the years. Typical examples of the model are seen here at Marble Arch, with London United's RML2519 leading Arriva's RML2686 into Oxford Street, wherein most Routemasters in London can be found. *Stephen Madden*

Left In spite of their extreme age – they date from 1959–65 – the standard original RM, albeit re-engined several times, is still in service in small numbers. Arriva and London Central are the principal operators of the type. RM275 in Whitehall on route 159 is a rare survivor with the original body style that featured plain non-opening front upper-deck windows. Although it no longer has an AEC engine under the bonnet, it still has its wind-down quarter-drop side windows. *Stephen Madden*

Left RM1082 of London Central has had a makeover, with 'hopper' windows fitted in place of the traditional style. Route 36 is one of a handful to feature limited route branding, on this vehicle carried alongside the blind boxes and above the side windows. From February 2003, this spot at Victoria also saw new route 436 taking over part of the frequency on the 36, using articulated vehicles. Some of the Routemasters were re-deployed to provide increased frequencies elsewhere. *Stephen Madden*

Facing page **Perhaps the most traditional of modern Routemaster liveries is that of Stagecoach, who use gold fleet numbers and rich cream relief bands, although this has been coupled with the latest fleetname style. Stagecoach has retained three of the former Green Line coach RMCs, with 57 deep-cushioned seats instead of the normal 64 of the standard RM. These are invariably mixed in with RMs and RMLs on route 15, and the enclosed platform doors often foil intending passengers used to jumping on board between stops! RMC1485 is alternatively numbered 12485 in the Stagecoach national fleet numbering scheme.** *Stephen Madden*

Above **The most unexpected event of recent times was the purchase back by TfL of several older RMs, redundant from other operators or from dealers and private owners. Marshalls of Cambridge headed up a refurbishment programme, and the first twenty-one of them went to Sovereign London in summer 2001 for route 13. Subsequently, other examples have been secured by TfL for service increases, especially for Arriva, and Arriva itself has refurbished some since the demise of Marshalls. All five Arriva routes (19, 38, 73, 137 and 159) have had increased requirements, and RM29 at Hyde Park Corner is one of those so allocated.** *Geoff Rixon*

Step-Entrance Double-Deckers

The buses from the late 1970s and 1980s period are fast disappearing from London service. Titans are down to penny numbers, the few Dominators have all gone, whilst handfuls of Metrobuses survive here and there, mostly as spare buses providing the increased pvr until new buses can be provided. The Leyland Olympian is mainly represented by the large fleet with Arriva, all based in south London, although most of them should be cleared away during 2003 as their routes are likely to be specified for new buses upon re-tender. The next generation dates from the 1988–1999 period. The Volvo B10M Citybus, Scania N113DRB, DAF DB250 and Dennis Arrow, none of which were very common in London anyway, have all seen their numbers reduced. On the other hand, the Volvo Olympian was a popular choice and all the large operators and a few of the smaller ones purchased some. Bodywork was largely shared between Northern Counties and Alexander, with a minority supplied by East Lancs. Alexander's R-type body and NC's Palatine I were upgraded to the Royale and Palatine II, and both styles were supplied concurrently. The last step-entrance double-deckers to be produced for London were CentreWest's twenty VNs for route 83 in March and April 1999.

Remarkable survivors are the handful of Titans which remained in service at the beginning of 2003. Blue Triangle has a number, used at times on routes 185 and 248, but London Central retains a few as spare cover. Spare they may be but throughout 2002 they were out in service every day, pending replacement. And so we find T1018 in Whitehall, crew operated on trunk route 12. *Stephen Madden*

Metrobuses also refuse to lie down. Compared with their contemporary vehicle the Titan, many more examples remain in service. It seems that as fast as new buses come to replace them, increased service levels around the network require them to hang on as spare cover. Metroline has the largest number, with about sixty left in passenger service. Although the company's route 240 remains a virtual 100% Metrobus operation, others can be found at all garages. M1208 performs a crew-operated journey on route 6, a service which has insufficient RMLs based at Willesden to cover its allocation. *Stephen Madden*

London United continues to hang on to any serviceable Metrobus for as long as possible, leading to M appearances on routes as diverse as the 9 and 220 at Hammersmith or the 406 and 411 into Surrey. M881 calls at Eden Street in Kingston on the 406 out to Epsom. Route 406 was of course a major country area route from Kingston out to Reigate and Redhill for several decades until Arriva gradually shortened it, reduced it, caused it to become unreliable, and finally abandoned it. *Geoff Rixon*

11

The Scania N113DRB is a rare type in London, only Metroline now having any in service. Ten Alexander bodied single-doored 78-seat examples (S11–20) are based at Potters Bar Garage, and operate mainly on routes 84, 242 and 310A into the outer northern suburbs of London. The 84 out to St Albans is a very old established service, and apart from during a few years in the 1980s has always been worked by red London buses. It once ran further south but now terminates at New Barnet. *Colin Brown*

Other than the last few examples of the Metrobus, and of course the Routemasters, the ECW-bodied Leyland Olympians of Arriva London South are the oldest vehicles still scheduled for all-day service in London, and they are concentrated on a few routes from Norwood, South Croydon and Thornton Heath Garages. Although some had received an internal refit some years ago, they tend to look somewhat dowdy nowadays. Route 2 still sees the type, and L207 travels up Park Lane. *Colin Brown*

The erstwhile Kentish Bus bought forty-three Northern Counties bodied Leyland Olympians, now numbered L514–556 by Arriva, in 1990 for tendered route successes in the Hackney area. The routes have changed, Kentish Bus has gone, and the vehicles all gravitated to Arriva and now are mostly at Barking and Norwood Garages. Barking's route 103 continues to be partly worked by this type of vehicle, and L529 traverses the back streets of Romford town centre. First London also have a few similar examples, single-doored and also inherited, in their case from London Buslines, and which are mostly used on route 158. *Gerald Mead*

Grey-Green was the proud winner of route 24 in 1988, and they bought some Alexander bodied Volvo B10M Citybuses, these continuing on the route once Arriva assumed responsibility for Grey-Green. More were bought for later tender wins and most survive with Arriva today, mostly at Barking Garage. Our picture shows Barking's VA121 at Romford Station. The B10M is a very high floor vehicle, and most operators have now disposed of them. A few other B10Ms but with East Lancs bodywork, operate with Arriva in the blue 'country' version of the livery on school services from Dartford, and just one in red (confusingly numbered L611) operates in the Croydon area and is normally to be found on route 403.
Colin Brown

Arriva is the present-day inheritor of a multiplicity of operators as the group has expanded and consolidated and, as far as London goes, has turned everything to red. Eleven Volvo Olympians with East Lancs bodies (now numbered L694–704) were new in 1994, and were inherited from the former London & Country fleet, where they had been in the two-tone green of that company. They are normally used on route 403, as epitomised by L697 at West Croydon Bus Station.
Stephen Madden

15

Some of the first examples of the Palatine II style from Northern Counties to be seen in London were the Volvo Olympians bought by London Suburban Bus in 1993/4 for their wins of routes 4 and 271, centred on Archway in north London. They were another operator to be taken over, in their case by Merseyside Transport, who later combined the routes with London Northern. That company was taken over by Metroline in 1998, which is how we come to see V201 on Waterloo Bridge in Metroline colours. The batch (V201–210/2–7) remains intact at Holloway Garage, and remain largely on the same two routes 4 and 271. *Mark Lyons*

The Volvo Olympian with Palatine II bodywork was chosen by CentreWest for both route 61 at Orpington in 1995 and for express route 607 in 1996, as V1–12 and V41–55. Both batches were single-doored, unusually for London, although it was a suitable choice for the routes concerned. In 2002, the 61 gained new buses and the 607 was increased in frequency, so some of those on the 61 were repainted and moved to Uxbridge, although they did retain their normal bus seats in contrast to the 'original 607s' which had high-backed seats. One of these was V10, passing through Ealing Broadway. Other Palatine II Olympians, coded NV161–187, are in stock with London General, and are spread over garages in south-west London. *Colin Stannard*

Having managed to dispose of its thirteen single-doored DBS class vehicles, DAF DB250s with Northern Counties bodywork, Arriva hung on to just two dual-doored versions, one of which (DBS15) was a former dealer stock vehicle. The other example, DBS14, was one of a batch of thirteen that had been bought in 1998 for route 85 (Kingston – Putney) and worked by Arriva's country garage at Leatherhead. They were passed to London United (as DN1–12) with the route, and later back to Arriva. Thus, two red ones work from Wood Green, normally on route 141, and both red and blue ones run into Bromley on Arriva's route 402 from far-off Tunbridge Wells.
Stephen Madden

The AV or the VA, when applied to a Volvo Olympian with Alexander bodywork are one and the same thing. The higher bodywork, the RH model, is an AV with Metroline and a VA with First London and London United (note that London United confusingly also use the VA code for the later Volvo B7TL). Similar bodywork, but to a slightly lower height (the RL model), is on Volvo Olympians of Stagecoach. These are also coded VA, but at the turn of 2002/3 most of these were being cascaded out of London. Yet another variation is on just nine with London Central, whose AV1–9 have high but single-door bodies of the Royale style, which simply has a modified frontal appearance. Our pictures depict the almost identical Metroline AV28 at Park Royal, and London United VA54 at Kingston, but note that the offside blank panel is in a different place, dependent on the staircase position.
Gerald Mead/Stephen Madden

The purchase of Metroline by the Singapore-based Delgro group resulted in one Volvo Olympian with Alexander Royale bodywork being repatriated to Britain. They would surely have liked to import more, but it was not to be and AV39 remains unique. There are several detail differences to the rest of Metroline's AV class (see opposite), but it fits in very well on routes 260 and 266. *David Stewart*

The NV or the VN are largely identical, both being Volvo Olympians with Northern Counties bodywork. Most of those in London are the standard Palatine I model, exemplified by First London VN104 nearing Golders Green. Those in use on route 83 were the very last step-entrance double-deckers to be delivered new to London in 1999. Similar buses with London Central and General are coded NV, whilst Metrobus also has identical vehicles (in the 817-829 and 859-896 blocks) operating mainly in their operating areas in Surrey and Sussex, but also appearing in towns such as Bromley and Croydon. *Colin Brown*

Typifying the common management of London Central and London General is this view of NV102 at Elephant & Castle. Many of General's routes at Sutton received new buses during 2002, and the Olympians at that garage were scattered to most other garages in the empire. Not only that, but several have moved around several times. At the time of this photograph, NV102 had transferred to Central at Camberwell, but retains General fleetnames. *Stephen Madden*

The East Lancs Pyoneer bodywork appears on Volvo Olympians of East Thames Buses and Metrobus. Those with East Thames (from the 338-372 batch) were inherited from Harris Bus early in 2000, but are gradually being replaced. Those at Metrobus (from the 830-858 batch) have operated mainly on routes 64 and 119, although some were being transferred elsewhere by the turn of 2002/3. The fine blue and yellow livery on No.853 at West Croydon provides a contrast to the slowly enveloping sea of red. *Stephen Madden*

Opposite During 1997/8 Capital Citybus took fifty-four Dennis Arrows into stock, of which 401-416 had Northern Counties bodywork and most of which have departed the fleet. The batch with East Lancs Pyoneer bodies (417-454) remains almost intact, and the majority are in the Capital red and yellow livery, although now under First London stewardship. At the beginning of 2003, most could be found on north London routes 76, 259 and 341, and No.452 is at High Holborn. The Arrows were allocated class codes AN or AE (this one should be AE452) but none have displayed those codes. *Mark Lyons*

Low-Floor Double-Deckers

This revolution in bus design was most abrupt, and there was virtually no gradual progression. The first low-floor double-deck buses to enter service in London were four of Arriva's DLAs on route 242 on 5th November 1998, and the last few step-entrance buses went into service just six months later. The subsequent drive to re-equip London's bus fleet in a relatively short time has seen around 2800 new low-floor buses coming into stock in a little more than four years. In contrast, in the whole of the UK outside London in that time, only around 1400 of the type has gone into service. There are notable exceptions such as Birmingham, Brighton and Edinburgh in particular, but some parts of the country, for example East Anglia, the south-west and Wales, have so far seen only penny numbers.

The first chassis type onto the scene was the DAF DB250LF, which was really an adaptation of the standard floor DB250 that had already been in production for some years. Over the next few years, Arriva ordered them in quantity, mostly with Alexander ALX400 bodywork, although some were received with Plaxton President bodies. The only other London operator to order the DB250LF was Capital Logistics, who requested six with Optare Spectra and ten with Plaxton President bodies. Both styles went onto route 60 in March 1999, but in late summer 2001 moved under London Buses auspices to Sovereign for route 114. This batch of buses is notable in that it includes the first Presidents to have entered service, and the only Spectras in London.

The Dennis Trident was next into service and, although the type was already running in Hong Kong, Stagecoach was the first London (and also the first UK) operator with its first ALX400 bodied example on route 55 on 25th January 1999. Metroline was next, with President-bodied examples beginning on route 43 on 19th April 1999. Indeed the ALX400 and President bodywork, in roughly equal proportions, became the main choice for the Trident over the next four years, although Blue Triangle and Metrobus took small batches with East Lancs Lolyne bodies.

Volvo's B7TL double-deck model came rather later, the first few to enter service being London Central's AVLs on route 63 on 28th January 2000, followed by route 45 three days later. As with the Trident, the ALX400 or President bodywork was the main choice, but a single example (VE953) came from East Lancs in October 2000 and was used intermittently by First London. London General bought fifty-two with East Lancs Myllennium Vyking bodywork in 2002. The principal change to the conformity came when the Wrightbus Eclipse Gemini arrived. The stylish vehicle was very different to what had gone before, and so far has been bodied only on the Volvo B7TL chassis. Arriva was first to get them, and the first example into service was on route 102 on 20th September 2001. Arriva will also be the first to take the Eclipse Gemini on the DAF DB250LF chassis during 2003.

All three types of chassis have come in short and long wheel-base versions, but the different ways of matching bodies with chassis has lead to slight variations in overall length, so the short ones work out as 9.9m–10.2m, the long ones 10.5m–10.8m. The low-floor design presented many problems not previously encountered, and largely centred over the staircase and door positions, and the incompatibility of London Buses' ideas with physical limitations. The effect was to have a low seating capacity on the lower deck and some wasted space on many earlier batches. Gradually over the years several common-sense changes have been made, and an improved layout is now standard.

Facing page **The newest body style to appear on London's double-deckers in 2002 was the East Lancs Myllennium Vyking, basically the Blackburn manufacturer's standard style but with an updated frontal styling. London General received fifty-two on 10.8m Volvo B7TL chassis, and all are allocated to Sutton Garage replacing Volvo Olympians on routes 93, 154 and 213. The first of the batch EVL1 travels along Eden Street in Kingston. The Myllennium styling is also applied to bodies built on other chassis, and the first ones for London on Trident chassis, and thus called 'Myllennium Lolyne' arrived in January 2003. These were for new route 388 with Hackney Community Transport, and adopted a new class code of HTL.** *Mark Lyons*

After taking only the longer (10.6m) DAF DB250LFs in 1998/9, most of those that followed to Arriva have been the shorter 10.2m version. Those with Alexander ALX400 bodywork are classified DLA, but there is no distinction made in class letters to denote which is short and which is long. DLA234 at Elephant & Castle is one of the shorter examples, distinguishable by the two half-width windows above the exit doors (the longer DLA has one full and one half-width window at that point). At Arriva the L in the class code denotes a low-floor bus. *Stephen Madden*

The first London operator of the Volvo B7TL was London Central, who took forty-six mainly for routes 45 and 63. They are classified AVL (Alexander-Volvo-low) as, in common with Arriva, London Central and General now use the letter L for a low-floor bus. However, this batch features the company's only ALX400 bodied vehicles thus far. AVL29 calls at the Bricklayers Arms in the Old Kent Road. *Geoff Rixon*

The combination of the Dennis Trident with ALX400 bodywork represents the largest single class of double-deck vehicle in London. Five operators share them, and all use a variation of the TA class code, but confusingly they do not all mean quite the same thing. Connex Bus, London United and Metroline use TA for the 9.9m version, but Stagecoach used TAS for the same type of vehicle. All have the standard six-bay upper-deck window arrangement. In Westminster, Connex Bus TA10 passes a group of demonstrators hoping to attract the attention of politicians in the Houses of Parliament. *Mark Lyons*

The longer version of the Trident/ALX400 combination has been called a plain TA by Stagecoach, but First and Metroline both use the more logical TAL. Both of the latter operators have only small batches (of 22 and 17 respectively), and have largely reverted to the Plaxton President for most subsequent deliveries. Metroline's TALs are normally concentrated on route 16, but TAL126 is seen at the southern end of route 32. The longer version is easily recognised by the small half-width window amidships. *Steve Maskell*

Stagecoach is by far the largest single operator of the Trident/ALX400 in London, and will have around 700 in stock by summer 2003. In the autumn of 2000 Stagecoach introduced a new national corporate colour scheme, and this view shows how it has been modified to suit TfL's 80%-red ruling. The advent of the new registration system in 2001 caused a crisis of identification, so Stagecoach started to add prominent fleet numbers to the front of the vehicle. TAS544 at Romford Market was altered to 17544s at the beginning of 2003, as part of the Stagecoach national re-numbering scheme. *Colin Brown*

Arriva has both long (10.6m) and short (10.2m) versions of the Plaxton President on DAF DB250LF chassis and, as with the DLA, the company does not differentiate between the two styles. DLP75 arrives at Trafalgar Square on route 29, one of the most frequent services in London. *Stephen Madden*

The Go-Ahead group's London Central and General companies have been enthusiastic supporters of the Volvo B7TL/Plaxton President combination. Even though they have bought alternative types as well, it has become the largest class in the companies' fleets. All thus far are 10.0m versions, and can be seen in all parts of the operating territory. Some of the newest of the PVL class went to Camberwell Garage, and PVL312 is seen displaying this rather unusual destination on route 45. *Stephen Madden*

Facing page **Both First and Metroline have short and long Tridents and Volvo B7TLs with President bodywork, and both use similar ways to differentiate them, with the letter L meaning long. First have TN, TNL,VT and VTL, and Metroline have TP, TPL, VP and VPL. London United has a batch of shorter Volvos as well, and they also use the VP classification. Route 9 is partly operated by these vehicles on Sundays, and VP123 is pictured in an off-route location at Temple Place, evidently on diversion away from the Strand.** *Mark Lyons*

Metroline's TP308 is a short Trident, and one of a batch introduced onto route 205, the first of the new routes introduced in central London, and running along the northern edge of the Congestion Charging Area. Most operators now specify gasket glazed windows rather than the bonded glazed style, to make it easier when windows need to be replaced. They can be recognised by their individual placing in the window line, plus the rounded corners mounted in rubber. *Colin Brown*

First London TNL1006 is a long Trident with President bodywork and, like all First's Presidents received up until autumn 2002, is fitted with bonded glazing. This has been superseded by gasket glazing on later deliveries. Crossing Holborn Viaduct on route 25, it shows the unusual blind style to denote the weekend route variation 'via Tower'. *Mark Lyons*

Not all operators used class codes, and Sovereign London received seventeen long Volvo B7TL/Presidents to upgrade the 183, one of several routes to revert to double-deckers in recent times. Originally numbered in a common series with other Blazefield group vehicles, the numbers were due to be altered in 2003 under new London United ownership. No.2727 travels through North Harrow. *Colin Stannard*

The Optare Spectra has never been a very common type, and the only ones now operating in London are a batch of six with Sovereign London, normally to be found on route 114. Unusually, the body style was built on both standard and low-floor chassis, habitually on the DAF DB250 series. Displaying '28', the remnant of an earlier classification of DLO28 when it was briefly with Arriva, this example is on a low-floor DAF chassis. The bus is calling at Shaftesbury Avenue in South Harrow. *Colin Brown*

First London's VE953 is a unique vehicle in London, and is most elusive as it has seen very little time in actual passenger service in its two years in stock. It was experimentally fitted with air conditioning, which has proved most troublesome. Allocated to Alperton Garage for route 79, it was caught here at Alperton Sainsbury's on a rare outing. It is a Volvo B7TL with a 10.2m East Lancs Vyking body. *Colin Brown*

The basic East Lancs Vyking design has been modified with frontal design changes into the 'Myllennium' style, and is fitted to London General's EVL class. An upper-deck 'climatic control system' is fitted to these vehicles and, in consequence, very few opening windows are provided – just two each side. EVL31 enters Wimbledon Bus Station on the trunk route 93. *Colin Brown*

Metrobus has been an enthusiastic supporter of East Lancs bodywork, and has followed its orders for bodies on Olympians with the East Lancs Lolyne on its two batches of Tridents. Routes 161 and 261 are the main places to find these machines, typified by No.417 in Bromley High Street. *Gerald Mead*

As with Metrobus, Blue Triangle has been a good customer for East Lancs Lolyne bodied Tridents, for its tender wins on routes 248 and 474. While Metrobus specified gasket glazed windows, Blue Triangle has the bonded glazed style. DL910 waits to depart from Romford Market on the 248. In January 2003 the DL class code was changed to TL. *Colin Brown*

As happened with the DAF/ALX400 combination in 1998, it was Arriva that was first to introduce the newest style of body, the Wrightbus Eclipse Gemini, to London streets in September 2001. By the turn of 2002/3 the production total had reached around 200, all so far on Volvo B7TL chassis, although some are due during 2003 on the DAF DB250LF. Arriva call them VLWs (Volvo-low-Wright), whilst London United use VR, London General WVL and East Thames VWL. Arriva's VLW45 calls at Edmonton 'Cambridge'. *Colin Brown*

London General's route 74 was the first of several central London routes to be split and shortened, although it still runs along Park Lane, where WVL21 is pictured, heading an NV on the same service. A protracted conversion of route 74 was in place over the autumn and winter of 2002/3. Many more of the same type are due during 2003, mainly to provide an enhanced service on the 133, to be split to the overlapping 133 and 333. *Colin Brown*

Over the turn of 2002/3, Arriva the Shires replaced the G- and H-registered Leyland Olympians on routes 142 and 340, whereon they had operated continuously for twelve years, by new DLAs. Well, they look the same as Arriva London's DLAs but they have a slightly different fleetname and fleet number. These are the first proper 'London red' buses for the Shires, and are DAF DB250LF with 10.1m ALX400 bodywork. Note that the TransBus badge by the headlight has replaced that of Alexander. No.6010 departs from Brent Cross.
Colin Brown

Armchair replaced all its Olympians on route 237, both H- and R-registered examples, in one fell swoop, at the beginning of January 2003. Together with the loss of those with the Shires on routes 142 and 340, the stock of Leyland bodied Olympians was almost eliminated from London Buses services. Armchair's choice is the Trident with TransBus ALX400 bodywork, and DT18 at Hounslow Heath carries the clever adaptation of the company's colours onto the standard London red livery.
Geoff Rixon

Step-Entrance Single-Deckers

This type of vehicle is fast disappearing from London routes, with large numbers sold off for provincial operation. Early Darts, in particular, have been a popular choice for small independent companies around the country, providing upgrades – in their eyes – on urban and rural routes once worked by coaches or minibuses. The Leyland National and its Greenway off-shoot, plus the more modern DAF/Optare Delta and MAN/Optare Vecta have all been withdrawn from passenger service, although some Deltas and Vectas are now used as driver trainers. There is one Dennis Lance, formerly a demonstrator, and First Essex normally use a couple of Lynxes on a school route in Romford. Twenty-four unusual Marshall-bodied MAN 11.220 buses date from 1996 and are normally found on Metroline route 46. The early Darts of the DT, DR,

DRL, DW, DWL classes, and even their follow-on classes such as the DNL, DP, DPL, DRN and EDR, are fast departing, with just about a dozen routes with Arriva, London General, Metrobus and Metroline still using them as their principal allocation.

On the minibus front, the legions of Ivecos, Renaults, Metroriders and Mercedes-Benz types that 'graced' our streets in the 1990s are now almost extinct in London. Those that remain in service are invariably on routes which are still awaiting a suitable low-floor minibus replacement or perhaps a route diversion to allow larger buses. Metroline has five MetroRiders and a Mercedes for routes H1/2/3, Crystals have some Mercedes on route R2, whilst the low-entry Varios are on routes U9 (Arriva), K9/K10 (Epsom), W12 (First) and 380 (Selkent).

One of the rarer classes of vehicle in London is the MAN 11.220 with Marshall bodywork, twenty-four of which were obtained by MTL London Northern in 1996. They are now the MM class with Metroline, and the majority are used on route 46, although due for replacement in 2003. A typical view, therefore, is of MM256 at King's Cross, amid the reconstruction work that has been a long-standing feature of that area. *Stephen Madden*

The Mercedes-Benz Vario was an attempt to provide a slightly lower entrance, but never really caught on in London. Routes K9, K10, U9 and W12 remain scheduled for the type at the beginning of 2003, and the 380 was in the process of conversion to Darts. Plaxton bodied No.2196 travels through Harefield on the U9. The route is operated by Arriva the Shires from their High Wycombe depot.
David Stewart

From around 300 MCW and Optare Metroriders, we are now down to single figures in London, with just two routes, Metroline H2 and Arriva Kent Thameside R5, still scheduled for the type. Arriva's No.1852 leaves Orpington Station on the R5, which is a fine circular rural ride around the North Downs of west Kent, once served from this same point by an earlier generation of midi-buses of the C class (Leyland Cubs) on route 471.
David Stewart

From the 200 Darts with Wright Handybus bodies of the DW/DWL classes obtained in London Buses days during 1990–93, just a few remain with First London, plus a couple with East Thames Buses used for training and ferry purposes. First hung on to their handful because of various route restrictions and late deliveries of replacements, and in January 2003 four were to inaugurate new route 323 in the Bow area until newer vehicles could be obtained. The former DW72 is now First 644 – as with other former Capital fleet vehicles, no class prefix is displayed – and it powers along Manford Way in Hainault. *David Stewart*

The Dennis Dart first appeared in 8.5m form in 1989, and was in production until 1997, since when the SLF has taken over completely. It got longer, and 9.0m versions of the DR and DW (as the DRL and DWL) were soon joined by small numbers of the DEL and DNL with East Lancs or Northern Counties bodies. The latter style is still represented in London on routes such as 214 and 274 with Metroline, who inherited them from MTL London Northern. Similar examples are at Enfield with Arriva and in metropolitan Kent with Arriva Kent Thameside, used on routes B11 and B13. DNL117 departs from Marble Arch back to Islington. *Stephen Madden*

Small numbers of step-entrance Darts, with the familiar Plaxton Pointer body, were still being delivered in 1996/7. Even though they are still fairly new, by comparison with provincial standards, most have already been replaced by newer SLF models. Some of the last to be built were two classes of 9.8m models, Arriva calling theirs LDR (i.e. a long DR) and Metroline EDR (extended DR). Representing both operators, we show two views at Southgate Station of LDR49 and EDR25. Both are identical, in spite of their classification, and the Arriva vehicle is one of a few that received the full-front cream livery style.
Stephen Madden/ Matthew Wharmby

Low-Floor Single-Deckers

These have been around rather longer than may be assumed. In 1993 London Buses ordered thirty-eight Dennis Lance SLFs and thirty Scania L113CRLs, all with Wright Pathfinder bodywork. They gradually went into service during 1994, some of the SLWs actually being delivered in the autumn of that year to Stagecoach after privatisation of the East London company. LLWs operated with CentreWest, London United and Metroline and, apart from the CentreWest ones that have been passed on to other companies in the West Country, the others are still in London on routes H91 and 186. Some of the SLWs have gone too, but those on route 101 remain on their original route.

The Dart SLF (SLF stood for super low floor, as it was a new concept at the time) first appeared at the Coach & Bus Show in October 1995, and the London Buses example exhibited there eventually went into experimental service with CentreWest in autumn 1996 registered P41 MLE. This pioneer SLF is still working in London, and is now with Thorpe's. It was Plaxton Pointer bodied, and this has proved to be the most popular choice for bodywork, and if one had to pick a 'typical UK single deck bus' then this is it. The Dart SLF now comes in five lengths, and has had six bodybuilders. Other than the Pointer, the Alexander ALX200 and Marshall Capital were the most popular, but both designs are now discontinued. The Wright Crusader and East Lancs Spryte only won small orders in London, while the Caetano Nimbus, the newest of the body designs on the Dart SLF, has been gaining prominence in 2001/2. Every London Buses route contractor save one – Crystals – operates Dart SLFs.

The Optare Excel gained several orders for London in the 1996-98 period, but no more have followed, and those remaining are due for replacement during 2003. On the other hand, the Optare Solo featured with Travel London (now part of Connex Bus) on route C1 during 1998, and these remained unique in London for three years until the model replaced older minibuses on routes B14, C3, K5 as well as on several 'Mobility Bus' services. The only true low-floor minibuses in London thus far are three 13-seater Mercedes-Benz Sprinters on First's route 395 through the restricted width Rotherhithe Tunnel.

Volvo has only a very minor presence in this sector, twenty-three B6BLEs with East Lancs bodies work routes 187/487, and three with Wright Crusader bodies on route H18. Just seven B10BLEs are with T-GM on route 726. One B7L with Wright Eclipse bodywork works on London Central's route 486 alongside the seventeen DAF SB220LCs with East Lancs Myllennium bodywork that had been originally bought to work routes to the Millennium Dome. DAF's new baby, the SB120 that was hoped to be a rival to the Dart SLF, has so far only won London orders from Arriva.

Scania had their new N94UB low-floor midibus 'launched' into London with London Easylink in late July 2002, when the first four of an order for fourteen went into service. The collapse of that operator caused withdrawal after less than four weeks, and the buses were stored. Eventually they were acquired by London Buses and put into service on the 42 with East Thames Buses at the end of 2002. Another venture was the Scania OmniCity, with the solitary London example going to Metrobus. However, at the end of 2002 it was back with Scania. Mercedes-Benz had not been widely known in the UK for its full-sized buses, but eleven Citaros were introduced by First on new route RV1 in central London on 27th April 2002. Then, thirty-one articulated versions followed for London General for routes 507 and 521 from 5th June 2002. Another sixty-five entered service early in 2003 on new route 436 with London Central and 453 with Stagecoach Selkent. All the articulated buses in London operate on an open boarding cash-less basis.

Opposite **Perhaps the 'big event' of 2002 was the introduction into London of the Mercedes-Benz Citaro, in both rigid and articulated forms. The rigid vehicles in use by First London on route RV1, which connects tourist sites south of the River with Covent Garden and The Tower, are 11.9m in length, and are decorated – above the windows – with drawings of places of interest on the route. Note the huge wing mirrors.** *Stephen Madden*

In the past there have been experiments with articulated buses in London, but the first mainstream operation began on 5th June 2002 on the two Red Arrow routes 507 and 521, when National Greenways were replaced by thirty-one Mercedes-Benz Citaro-G vehicles. They have a stated capacity of 49 seated and 91 standing. In February 2003 two more routes (436 and 453) will join them, using similar vehicles. If pronouncements from TfL and politicians are to be followed by actions, then many more of the same are likely to appear on London's streets. MAL2 shows off its impressive 18-metre length outside the Prudential building in Holborn. *Mark Lyons*

In contrast to the 11.9m Citaro and 18m Citaro-G, Mercedes-Benz also has the honour of having provided the smallest capacity bus on any London bus route. Just 7.1m in length with just thirteen seats – but with low-floor wheelchair access – three little Koch-bodied Sprinters work the 395 from Limehouse to Surrey Quays through the Rotherhithe Tunnel. ES799 approaches Canada Water Station in the first view and Rotherhithe in the second.
Colin Stannard/Phillip Wallis

London Buses was in the forefront of experimentation with early low-floor buses in 1993/4, well before they became a standard product. They sponsored trials on five routes with batches of Dennis Lance SLF and Scania N113CRL, both carrying Wright Pathfinder bodies. Two of those routes still use the same types to this day, although the vehicles have since adopted company liveries. Thus we see Lance LLW30 at Edgware on route 186, and Scania SLW24 at Wanstead on route 101, still plying their trade. *Stephen Madden/Mark Lyons*

The Caetano Nimbus body was developed in 2000, and London's first examples went to Hackney Community Transport for route 153, and Blue Triangle (368), Docklands Buses (167). Mitcham Belle (152 and 493) and T–GM (routes H25, 465 and 235) have followed. The latest recruit is First London, who has ordered a fair number for service during 2003. The attractive Blue Triangle livery adorns this nicely proportioned DN186 at Barking. *Geoff Rixon*

Arriva is so far the only operator in London to take the DAF SB120/Wrightbus Cadet. Most are red and are deployed on routes 184, 298, 313 and 319, while another fourteen are blue and operate routes 256 and 346 from Grays Garage. There are three different lengths, most being 10.2m, although three 9.4m are on the 346, and seven, like DWL29 depicted here in Chingford, are 10.8m for route 313. *Colin Stannard*

There are many bodywork variations on the Dart SLF, but some remain quite rare, perhaps the rarest being the eight with Wright Crusader bodies, which can be found on London United route 440. CD6 turns from Twyford Avenue onto the Uxbridge Road at Acton. *Colin Stannard*

Just two operators in London use the East Lancs Spryte bodied Dart SLF, First London having thirteen on route S2 serving Stratford. The other seven are with Wing's Buses in farthest west London, of which three are in yellow and orange for route U7, and four in two-tone green for route H50. Somewhat unhelpfully but not unusually, we see a vehicle nicely branded for the H50 in use on the U7. *Colin Brown*

Limebourne bought 34 Dart SLFs with 10.7m Caetano Compass bodywork in 1999, principally for routes 42, 156 and 344. The 42 was later lost, and the other two routes passed – with the whole company operation – to Connex Bus, and have since been converted to Trident operation. The DCLs, as they were dubbed, remained in limbo for a time, until some were acquired by East Thames Buses, who now use them mainly on route 108. The former DCL435, now number-less, approaches Lewisham. *Mark Lyons*

Opposite The infamous Millennium Dome spawned new and altered bus services, and London Central received seventeen DAF SB220LFs with air-conditioned 12-metre East Lancs bodywork for special routes M1 and M2. After closure of the Dome, the buses were re-deployed to new route 486, still to the Dome (or North Greenwich Station as it is now more properly known), but running through from Bexleyheath. MD9 is one of three with roof mounted gas fuel tanks. *Gerald Mead*

The Dennis Dart SLF is quite simply the standard low-floor single-deck bus in London, and comes in every variety of length, body style and door arrangement. Half-a-dozen London operators chose the attractive Alexander ALX200 body, although production has now been discontinued. Stagecoach, Connex and Epsom Buses have examples of the shortest 8.9m version, and Connex Bus DA1 calls at Vauxhall before reconstruction work on a transport interchange began. Most have the intermediate 10.2m version, but Arriva has a batch of the longest 10.8m vehicles, usually to be found on route 407, epitomised by ADL21 at West Croydon. *Mark Lyons/Geoff Rixon*

The Marshall Capital bodied Dart SLF has achieved over 600 examples in the London fleets, although some of the earliest ones have now been 'cascaded' by First. The vast majority came to the First Group fleets, classified DM, DML and DMS for 9.3m, 10.2m and 8.9m versions, and they are spread over the company's network. DMS349 stops in Tottenham High Road on the short and infrequent local 318 route. In recent times, First has added Rail and Underground symbols to place names on its blinds, and both are featured here. *Colin Stannard*

Other Marshall Dart SLFs were shared between Metroline and London Central/General. Confusingly, both also used DMS and DML, and both differed in some respects from the codes used by First. At Metroline DMS was a 9.3m and DML a 10.2m model, but at London Central DMS was 8.9m and DML the 9.3m model. In this view, DML12 arrives in Whitehall on route 139, a service which is due for double-decking and extension to Waterloo during 2003. *Stephen Madden*

One of the newest low-floor types is the Scania N94UB, fourteen of which were ordered by Durham Travel Services for route 42. The vehicles, with East Lancs Myllennium bodywork, were subsequently bought by London Buses after the demise of DTS. ELS 11 is seen at Denmark Hill. *David Stewart*

The ubiquitous Dart SLF with a Plaxton Pointer body is without doubt the standard single-deck bus in London. Most operators use them, and they can be found in all parts of London. The majority of the longer ones are dual-doored, but almost all of the shorter ones are single-doored, otherwise very few seats would be available! This picture selection depicts four of the smaller operators, and four different lengths. Looking at the offside of the vehicle, and ignoring the rearmost pair of small windows, the length can be determined by the window arrangement. There is one further length in London, not illustrated here, that being the ultra-long 11.3m version, just a batch of thirteen being used on Stagecoach route 227 at Bromley. The 8.8m body has four-and-a-half windows, shown on Wing's Buses SK02TZT at Hayes Station. The manufacturer has a marketing name for this version, the 'MPD' (Mini Pointer Dart). The 9.3m body has five windows, Sovereign London having just five of these specifically for route 398. No.559 is turning out of Currey Road, Greenford, wherein a 'bus gate' activated by a key is situated. The 10.1m body has five-and-a-half windows, and is the most popular choice of length. Thorpes DLF88 is at Brent Park, Neasden, on route 316 which was taken over from Metroline in October 2002. The 10.7m body has six windows, and here we see Mitcham Belle's No.008 in Streatham. Later Pointer Darts with the company have been 10.1m models, and they have since turned to the Nimbus.

Mark Lyons, Colin Stannard, Geoff Rixon, Gerald Mead

We cannot possibly illustrate every variant of the Pointer Darts, but two more operators and nearside views are now featured. Armchair introduced fleet numbers during 2001 and a new red-based livery in 2002. The orange, white and black colours of the company's house style have been incorporated on DP1019, a 10.1m dual-doored Pointer travelling through Ealing Broadway. *Colin Stannard*

Tellings-Golden Miller have most of their fleet in their house colours, even though Darts delivered since summer 2002 have been in a red-based style. The company operates astride the London/Surrey border, and a mixture of London Buses, Surrey Council, commercial and contract routes serve Kingston. Operating totally within the Royal Borough are some services for Kingston University students, and it looks as though the 10.7m length has been fully utilised – and more – in this shot of a packed No.517. *Colin Brown*

The Optare Excel is now a very rare type in London, as operators withdraw and sell them. London United has six, meant for route 110, and East Thames Buses has a few left of those inherited from Harris Bus, usually on route 132. For just one year, Tellings-Golden Miller is running route 216 between Kingston and Staines, although it is due to revert to London United in summer 2003, and the small batch of Optare Excels inherited from Capital Logistics usually maintain this route. *Colin Brown*

Six operators in London – so far – use the Optare Solo, and all used on normal service are the shorter M850 (i.e. 8.5m) model. Connex Bus use them on routes C1 and C3, Crystals (B14 and R6), Epsom Buses (S4 and S7). Mitcham Belle (K5) and First Essex (193), while Crystals and Thorpes have two each for mobility bus duties. Crystals have a couple of the longer 9.2m versions for their mobility work. Both Epsom Buses and Crystals have adopted all-red liveries, and Crystals' Y295PDN crosses the Sidcup by-pass on route B14.
Colin Stannard

First in Essex has completely submerged the former Thamesway livery on route 193, when its yellow and purple Mercedes-Benz 709s were replaced by new Optare Solos in March 2002, in a red livery indistinguishable from other First vehicles in London. This is a good example of how the large groups are gradually consolidating their operations and liveries. Having said that, No.505 is still attributed to First in Essex, and calls ar South Street, Romford.
Mark Lyons

A unique type in London is the batch of seven Volvo B10BLEs with Alexander ALX300 bodywork in use by Tellings-Golden Miller on limited-stop route 726 between Heathrow and Bromley. Indeed they are the only ALX300s in London. No.902 is an example of this large vehicle, at 12m in length and with 44 seats and luggage racks. *Stephen Madden*

A batch of three vehicles with Arriva the Shires is unique in London service, these being Volvo B6BLEs with Wrightbus Crusader bodywork, and used on route H18. The route performs a sort of a crescent shape around Harrow, and No.3258 is seen in Harrow Weald. *David Stewart*

Twenty-three Volvo B6BLEs with East Lancs Spryte bodywork operate on routes 187 and 487 in west London. Delivered new to Metropolitan Omnibus, that company's routes and buses were taken over by Thorpes on 1st November 2002. Within a few weeks, most had received Thorpes yellow bands and fleetnames, as shown on VS513 in Whitton Avenue West. *Haydn Davies*

Tellings-Golden Miller adopted a dual sourcing policy for bodies on its newer Darts, taking Pointers as well as an increasing number of Caetano Nimbuses. During summer 2002 a new red based livery was adopted for buses on London Buses routes. All three company colours, white, blue and gold, were incorporated, but unfortunately the gold does not sit easily on the red background. This view depicts Pointer No.435 at Surbiton heading for Dorking Townfield Court, which now occupies the site of the former Country bus garage. *David Stewart*

Miscellaneous Operations

Not everything in the world of London's buses is on a mainstream TfL contract route. Arriva's Leaside Travel division has a fair quantity of Metrobuses on school and contract work, these being in an unusual purple and white based livery. Leaside Travel also has fifteen coaches for excursion and private hire work, while Metroline and Stagecoach each maintain a couple of coaches as well. Several other LB contractors have separate coach fleets, Armchair, Epsom Coaches and Tellings-Golden Miller being prominent in this regard.

Many small independent companies specialise in weekend rail replacement work around London, although the vehicles are normally used on school or country service work outside Greater London during the week. Metrobuses and Titans, many of them former London examples, feature prominently. Principal companies include Anglia Bus, Carousel Buses, Ensign Bus, Imperial, Legg's, Northdown, Regal, Redroute, Southlands, Sullivan Buses, Thames Bus, Town & Country, Trustline and Z&S of Aylesbury. Of these, Northdown run a few non-TfL services into Greater London, and Sullivan Buses is to gain its first TfL contract route later in 2003. Some of these operators have helped out on TfL services such as on route 185, after Durham Travel ceased operation in August 2002. Other companies operate non-TfL services into the periphery of the Greater London county to points such as Uxbridge (First Beeline) and Romford (First Essex), while some TfL contractors also run commercial or county council routes to just outside Greater London to places such as Staines, Watford or Epsom.

There are several vehicles in special or historic liveries, such as Stagecoach with RMC1461 in old Green Line colours and which often appears on route 15. They have also kept their original Titan T1 as a preserved vehicle. Open-top RMC1510 is kept by First for private hire work but sometimes turns out on route 23. London United has RML880 in a copy of a pre-war livery, and it is often on routes 9 or 94. This RML actually displays its original fleet number ER880 that it carried when

new in 1961. London Central and General have eight buses in various versions of old liveries, but are mostly only on special duties. Arriva has an AEC Regent V and other operators have one or two Routemasters, including the odd open-topper, kept for private hire and special occasions. Then there are the driver trainers, and plenty of Metrobuses and even a handful of Titans can be found in such use throughout London. One historic vehicle kept for training by Metroline is M1, which was London's first Metrobus back in 1978. London United withdrew from passenger service all eight of its Vectas and Stagecoach all its Deltas, and these are now used only on training duties.

Above right **Arriva's private hire and contract arm Leaside Travel operate a fair number of Metrobuses in this unusual maroon based livery. Each schoolday, around 25 of them work special journeys in and around north London for London Buses. Most of these journeys are numbered in the 600 series, but some follow normal bus routes and thus take the parent route number. Thus we see M1332 at Neasden on route 232, a service otherwise operated by Metroline throughout the week.** *Geoff Rixon*

In times of crisis, whether planned or unplanned, all sorts of operators from inside and outside London are called upon to help out. Most planned occurrences are on rail replacements, and it is there that many ex-London Ms and Ts are often to be found. An unplanned occurrence was the demise of Durham Travel, and at the beginning of 2003 several operators, including Redroute Buses of Gravesend pictured here at Victoria with M1229, were still covering route 185 until the contract could be formally re-awarded to a new operator. *Stephen Madden*

All the larger London operators keep some of their fleet, often older members, for driver training, although private training schools are also called upon to assist. The Metrobus is the most popular vehicle on these duties, and it is customary practice to paint them in a form of eye catching or brighter livery. Arriva has a rather plain white and grey on M1129 at Aldwych, while London United has gone for yellow (some other Ms have orange) crescents seen on M46 crossing Kingston Bridge. *Geoff Rixon*

Not everything is red in central London, and Arriva has three 8.8m Pointer Darts on a frequent link between offices and hospitals in the Waterloo and Westminster area, this being a contract for the DSS. PDL16 cruises around the Elephant & Castle, the only clue to its Arriva ownership being the corporate 'swirl' logo in the blind box.
Stephen Madden

Some operators have one or two vehicles in traditional style or historic liveries, and these can usually be seen on normal bus services, although they tend to be kept back when there is a special occasion to celebrate. Stagecoach East London has restored RMC1461 to its original 1962 Green Line livery, and the bus rounds Marble Arch on a trip to Paddington on route 15.
Geoff Rixon

The London United services 555/6/7 from Heathrow to Ashford, Sunbury, Walton and Chertsey cross the London border, but are actually Surrey County Council contracts. South of Sunbury they now cover what were once red London bus routes with RFs and BLs. Eleven long Dart SLF/Pointers (DP23–33) maintain the services in this unusual route branded livery, and DP28 is on the Bath Road on Heathrow North Side.
Stephen Madden

When London Buses retracted their red bus operations back from South Mimms in February 2002, Hertfordshire County Council sponsored a new 398 service to cover, and took the opportunity to restore a direct link between Potters Bar and Borehamwood at the same time. Local operator Sullivan Buses won the contract, and one of their attractive 9.2m Dart SLF/Caetano Nimbuses, DN3, is pictured here. During 2003, Sullivan Buses are due to operate their first London Buses contract (383) in the Barnet area. *Colin Brown*

Sightseeing Buses

Two main operators, Arriva and Big Bus, now provide sightseeing services, and each field around eighty buses. Arriva's sightseeing buses are based mainly at Wandsworth Garage and the fleet includes over fifty ex-London Metrobuses, a few closed top but most converted to open top. There are seventeen high-capacity MCW Metroliners and eleven former Hong Kong tri-axle Metrobuses. Big Bus Company also has ten similar former Hong Kong Metrobuses. The rest, though, are more historic, in that about thirty DMS class Fleetlines and thirty Titans are owned, all fully or partially open-topped. Three Big Bus Routemasters are often to be found parked at main pick-up points, but are rarely used in service.

A series of ownership changes has resulted in LT's 'Original Tour' of London passing, via London Coaches, to Arriva. A more recent link saw Ensign combine its own 'London Pride' tours with those of Arriva. The vehicle fleet is virtually entirely Metrobus, both ex-LT Ms and former China Motor Bus tri-axle models, and using MB and EMB class codes. The Original Tour livery is based on the Arriva style, but with a larger cream 'scoop' at the front as seen on MB351 at Monument. *Stephen Madden*

The 'City Sightseeing' brand is from the Ensign operation and is seen on MB558 just about to cross London Bridge. *Stephen Madden*

Arriva's City Sightseeing fleet also has several MCW Metroliners and, unlike the tri-axle Metrobuses obtained from Hong Kong, these had been converted to open-top after a previous career on National Express work. A mid-summer view of well-loaded ML28 on London Bridge shows how useful these vehicles have become to the tourist industry. *David Stewart*

The Fleetline, a stalwart type of the 1970s, never had a happy period with London Transport, and most of them had a relatively short life on ordinary bus services. However, plenty went on to lengthy careers with other operators around the UK and abroad. The only London operator of the type nowadays is Big Bus Company, who has about three dozen on sightseeing work, typified by the former DMS1958 rounding Marble Arch. The yellow shirted tour guide is performing his live commentary. *Geoff Rixon*

The Big Bus Company has arguably some of the best turned out buses in London, and has invested in Titans in a big way for its tours of London. Not only that, it also has a quantity of former China Motor Bus tri-axle Metrobuses. Virtually the whole Big Bus fleet is open-topped, some vehicles only partially, while some Titans can have a canvas awning put across the roof when necessary. Titan CRM1792 (ex T792) is in Park Lane and ML764 at Trafalgar Square. *Stephen Madden*

Fleet Numbering and Class Codes

London Buses and its antecedents have used vehicle type codes to identify its classes ever since the LGOC introduced such vehicles as the B, K and S types in the first quarter of the 20th Century. Following privatisation of the London Buses companies in 1994/5, each proceeded with its own system or, more correctly, each modified, adapted and expanded on those that went before. Inevitably, differing ideas on how to denote a type variation has caused some anomalies between companies, and these practices have led to some confusion to the uninitiated. Until about 1986, the world was simple, London Transport buses were numbered in large classes, and the red buses continued to be so numbered through into the 1990s. Most of the smaller operators entering the London bus arena, following route tendering in the 1980s and 1990s, did not use class letters, although as time has moved on, some – for example, Armchair and Epsom Buses, and later entrants such as Connex Bus – have adopted them. Others used a plain numerical fleet numbering sequence, but even here one or two that didn't, such as Mitcham Belle and Tellings-Golden Miller, have since adopted such a system.

To take some examples of potential confusion, AVs and VAs can both be Alexander bodied Volvo Olympians, NVs and VNs (and a few of Arriva's Ls) are all outwardly identical Northern Counties bodied Olympians. Five operators use the TA code for Alexander bodied Tridents, but Metroline, Connex Bus and London United use TA for short versions, and Stagecoach uses TA for long ones. First don't have any TA buses as such, but they do have TALs, i.e. long ones. Metroline also uses TAL for long versions of the TA, but Stagecoach uses TAS for short ones. Metroline has perhaps the most logical arrangement, and their large fleet of Plaxton President bodied double-deckers is classified TP, VP, TPL, VPL for Trident (T) or Volvo (V) chassis, with the P for Plaxton and L simply denoting the longer version. First is similar, with TN, VT, TNL, VTL for Trident (T) or Volvo (V) chassis, but with the N signifying not Plaxton but Northern Counties, recalling the former owner's name for the Wigan factory that produces the President. Having used VN already for Volvo Olympian/ Northern Counties, the introduction of Volvo B7TL/Presidents resulted in another code (T) being 'invented', resulting in VT and VTL, otherwise VN would have denoted two different types of bus!

The letter D can perhaps mean a Dart, a DAF or even a dual-doored bus, while a letter L usually means low or long, but rarely in the same company! At Arriva, after L (for Leyland) Olympian, and then LDR (for long Dart), the letter L on modern vehicles (since 1997) now signifies a low-floor bus.

The letter L is for a low-floor bus at London Central and General, but at First and Metroline L denotes a longer version. The differences between short, very short, medium and long can be quite important in a garage's daily vehicle allocation, and First, Metroline and London United all have differing class codes to show the variations. Nevertheless, London Central and General have plenty of LDPs (low-floor Dart Plaxton) but they are of four different lengths. Arriva has both short and long versions of the DLA and DLP (DAF low-floor Alexander or Plaxton) and various lengths of the PDL (Plaxton Dart low-floor). London General also have a PDL code, but there it is on a double-decker, being the Plaxton Dennis (Trident) low-floor, following the precedent set by the AVL, PVL and EVL for Alexander, Plaxton or East Lancs Volvo (B7TL) low-floor double-deckers.

Stagecoach went one further with its SLD (super low-floor Dart), which came in five different lengths and was mixed up with either Alexander ALX200 or Plaxton Pointer bodywork. During 2002, Stagecoach indulged in a re-classification of all SLDs to DL, DM, DS and DSS codes. This attention to detail was short-lived as, from 6th January 2003 the whole national Stagecoach fleet, including London, adopted a combined five-digit scheme. However, Stagecoach continued to refer to some of its buses by class code suffix letters. First began a national numbering scheme during 2002, but this was slow to develop. However, it is likely to reach London in 2003.

Perhaps the most bizarre event of recent times concerns the latest Volvo B7TL/ Wright Eclipse Gemini vehicles. Virtually identical vehicles of three operators use the same three letters but as an anagram, so we have VLW (Arriva), WVL (London General) or VWL (East Thames Buses). London United had three of these buses, but have called them VR – is that Wright? There are many examples of differences to be found, and these are highlighted in the tables that follow.

Three operators have current vehicles with a mixture of old (numbers only) and new (class codes) fleet identities, and Stagecoach has a combination of new numbers and old class codes. First in London has generally adopted the CentreWest class codes, but has invented several new ones to encompass the former Capital Citybus fleet. Confusingly, most of these vehicles are known within the company by their class codes, but in many cases they are not displayed on the vehicles themselves. Additionally, several of the contract operators mentioned in the 'miscellaneous vehicles' section of this book use either class codes inherited or adapted from LT systems, some of their own, or none at all. These are outside the scope of this book.

TfL contract operators using class letters: Armchair; Arriva London; Blue Triangle; Connex Bus; Epsom Buses (Quality Line); Hackney Community Transport; London Central; London General; London United; Metroline; Thorpes. Additionally, sightseeing buses of Arriva and Big Bus have class letters.

TfL contract operators using a mix of class codes and plain numbers: East Thames Buses; First in London; Sovereign London; Stagecoach in London.

TfL contract operators using only plain numbering systems: Arriva Southern Counties, including Kent Thameside and Kent & Sussex, plus TfL routes from Grays; Arriva the Shires & Essex; First in Essex; Metrobus; Mitcham Belle; Tellings-Golden Miller.

TfL contract operators with no fleet numbering systems: AirLinks; Crystals; Docklands Buses; Wing's Buses. These operators have only very small numbers of buses on TfL duties. Wing's used to use WB codes for its earliest Darts, but these have now been abandoned.

Numerical systems or non-numbered systems, listed in company order

Note that where batches of numbers are quoted, these are not necessarily complete batches. An asterisk denotes any numbers or letters within the batch.

AirLinks T71–76WWV (Dennis Dart SLF/Plaxton Pointer 2 10.7m)

Arriva Southern Counties Vehicles on TfL services come from Dartford, Grays, Northfleet and Tunbridge Wells depots. Buses are numbered in groups, prefixed 1*** for midibuses (mostly MetroRiders), 3*** for most single-deck buses (Dart/Northern Counties, Dart SLF/Plaxton are seen in Greater London), 45** for DAF SB120/Wrightbus Cadets (from Grays), 62** for DAF DB250/ Northern Counties Palatine II (into Bromley), 77** (Volvo B10M/East Lancs double-deckers).

Arriva the Shires & Essex Also a group numbering system, 2*** midibuses (including Mercedes-Benz Varios), 3*** single-deck (including Dart SLF/Plaxton or Alexander ALX200, and 3258–60 Volvo B6BLE/Wrightbus Crusader), 4*** coaches, 5*** double-deck (including Leyland or Volvo Olympian/ Northern Counties or Leyland, MCW Metrobuses), 6*** (DAF DB250LF/Alexander ALX400).

Crystals N6**JGP, S1**HGX (Mercedes-Benz 709D/711D/811D), W4**CWX, Y2**PDN, YJ51JWW (Optare Solo).

Docklands Buses HV02OZ* or PC*/PD* (Dennis Dart SLF/Caetano Nimbus 10.5m).

East Thames Buses all in 3** series, including Optare Excel, Volvo Olympian/East Lancs Pyoneer.

First in Essex 501–511(Optare Solo), 14** (Leyland Lynx), 852-5 (Dennis Dart SLF/Marshall).

Metrobus 2** and 3** (Dennis Dart SLF/Plaxton Pointer (all lengths), 4** (Dennis Trident/East Lancs Lolyne), 451+(Scania Omni-Dekka), 513 (Scania OmniCity), 7** (Dennis Dart/Plaxton Pointer), 8** (Leyland or Volvo Olympian/Leyland or Northern Counties Palatine I or East Lancs Pyoneer).

Mitcham Belle 001-046 (Dennis Dart SLF/Plaxton Pointer 2), 047–049 (MCW Metrobus), 050-2/7 (Optare Solo), 063-6/8–083 (Dennis Dart SLF/Caetano Nimbus).

Sovereign London 24–29 (DAF DB250LF/Optare Spectra), 30-39 (DAF DB250LF/Plaxton President), 48-64 (Leyland or Volvo Olympian/Northern Counties Palatine I, 503–562 (Dennis Dart SLF/Plaxton Pointer 2), 2717-33 (Volvo B7TL/Plaxton President 10.6m). This fleet is in the process of gaining fleet class codes, and some types are also included in the main lists above.

Stagecoach in London A new national numbering scheme commenced in January 2003, and this covers the following batches in London – 12***(Routemasters), 16***(Volvo Olympian/Alexander RL or Northern Counties Palatine I (all lengths), 17***(Dennis Trident/Alexander ALX400 (all lengths), 23***(Mercedes-Benz Citaro-G), 26***(DAF SB220/Optare Delta), 286**(Scania N113CRL/Wright Pathfinder), 333**(Dennis Dart SLF/Alexander ALX200), 34***(Dennis Dart SLF/Plaxton Pointer 2 or Alexander ALX200(all lengths), 42***(Mercedes-Benz Vario/Plaxton Beaver), 52***(Volvo coaches). The former class codes may be seen on some buses, and details of these are retained in the class coding tables that follow.

Tellings-Golden Miller Numbers under 99 (Various minibuses, mostly Mercedes-Benz types), 301–338 (Dennis Dart SLF/Plaxton Pointer 2 8.8m), 401–420, 434-445 (Dennis Dart SLF/Plaxton Pointer 2 10.1m), 421-433 (Dennis Dart SLF/Caetano Nimbus 10.5m) or 613-633 (11.0m), 501–519, 601–612 (Dennis Dart SLF/Plaxton Pointer 10.6m or Pointer 2 10.7m), 701-708,748-758 (Mercedes-Benz Vario/Plaxton Beaver), 901-907 (Volvo B10BLE/Alexander ALX300).

Wing's Buses V3**MBV, W4**CRN (Dennis Dart SLF/East Lancs Spryte 10.3m), SK02T** (Dennis Dart SLF/Plaxton Pointer 2 8.8m).

CLASS LETTERS

Double-deck buses (all categories)

AE	Dennis Arrow/East Lancs Pyoneer (First).
AN	Dennis Arrow/Northern Counties Palatine II (First).
AV	Volvo Olympian/Alexander Royale (London Central, also Metroline AV39 only).
AV	Volvo Olympian/Alexander RH (Metroline).
AVL	Volvo B7TL/Alexander ALX400 10.1m (London Central).
CRM	Leyland Titan (with convertible roof) (Big Bus).
DBS	DAF DB250RS/Northern Counties Palatine II (Arriva).
TL	Dennis Trident/East Lancs Lolyne 10.0m (Blue Triangle).
DLA	DAF DB250LF/Alexander ALX400 10.2m or 10.6m (Arriva).
DLO	DAF DB250LF/Optare Spectra (Sovereign).
DLP	DAF DB250LF/Plaxton President 10.2m or 10.6m (Arriva, Sovereign).
DW	DAF DB250LF/Wrightbus Eclipse Gemini (for Arriva in 2003).
DM	Daimler or Leyland Fleetline (Big Bus).
DT	Dennis Trident/Alexander ALX400 9.9m (Armchair).
EM	Leyland Titan (Big Bus).
EMB	MCW Metrobus tri-axle (Arriva TOLST).
HTL	Volvo B7TL/East Lancs Myllennium Vyking 10.8m (London General).
L	Leyland Olympian/ECW or Alexander RH (Arriva).
L	Leyland Olympian/Northern Counties Palatine I (Arriva).
L	Leyland Olympian/Leyland (Sovereign).
L	Volvo Olympian/East Lancs (Arriva L694–704).
L	Volvo B10M Citybus/East Lancs (Arriva L611 only).
LL	Leyland Olympian/Leyland (First LL250 only).
LN	Leyland Olympian/Northern Counties (First).
M	MCW Metrobus.
MB	MCW Metrobus (Arriva TOLST).
MCW	MCW Metrobus (Blue Triangle).
ML	MCW Metroliner (Arriva TOLST).
ML	MCW Metrobus tri-axle (Big Bus).
OM	MCW Metrobus open-top (London Central/London General).
NV	Volvo Olympian/Northern Counties Palatine I or II (London Central/London General).
PDL	Dennis Trident/Plaxton President 9.9m (London Central/London General).
PVL	Volvo B7TL/Plaxton President 10.0m (London Central/London General).
RM	AEC Routemaster/Park Royal 27ft 6in (some have been modified by Marshalls).
RMC	AEC Routemaster/Park Royal 27ft 6in Green Line coach version.
RMF	AEC Routemaster/Park Royal 30ft, front entrance version (Big Bus).
RML	AEC Routemaster/Park Royal 30ft.
RV	AEC Regent V/Park Royal (Arriva RV1 only).
S	Scania N113DRB/Alexander RH (Metroline).
T	Leyland Titan.
TA	Dennis Trident/Alexander ALX400 9.9m (London United, Connex, Metroline)
TA	Dennis Trident/Alexander ALX400 10.5m (Stagecoach).
TAL	Dennis Trident/Alexander ALX400 10.5m (First, Metroline).
TAS	Dennis Trident/Alexander ALX400 9.9m (Stagecoach).
TN	Dennis Trident/Plaxton President 9.9m (First).
TNL	Dennis Trident/Plaxton President 10.5m (First).
TP	Dennis Trident/Plaxton President 9.9m (Metroline)
TPL	Dennis Trident/Plaxton President 10.5m (Metroline).
V	Volvo Olympian/Northern Counties Palatine II (First, Metroline).
VA	Volvo B10M Citybus/Alexander RV (Arriva).
VA	Volvo Olympian/Alexander RH (First, London United).
VA	Volvo Olympian/Alexander RL (Stagecoach).
VA	Volvo B7TL/Alexander ALX400 10.1m (London United).
VE	Volvo B10M Citybus/East Lancs (Arriva).
VE	Volvo B7TL/East Lancs Vyking (First VE953 only).
VFL	Volvo B7TL/Alexander ALX400 10.6m (First).
VLW	Volvo B7TL/Wrightbus Eclipse Gemini 10.1m (Arriva).
VN	Volvo Olympian/Northern Counties Palatine I (First, Stagecoach).
VP	Volvo B7TL/Plaxton President 10.0m (London United, Metroline).
VPL	Volvo B7TL/Plaxton President 10.6m (Metroline).
VR	Volvo B7TL/Wrightbus Eclipse Gemini 10.1m (London United).
VT	Volvo B7TL/Plaxton President 10.0m (First).
VTL	Volvo B7TL/Plaxton President 10.6m (First).
VWL	Volvo B7TL/Wrightbus Eclipse Gemini 10.6m (East Thames Buses).
WVL	Volvo B7TL/Wrightbus Eclipse Gemini 10.1m (London Central/London General).

Single-deck buses (all categories)

ADL	Dennis Dart SLF/Alexander ALX200 10.2m or 10.8m (Arriva).
CD	Dennis Dart SLF/Wright Crusader 10.2m (London United).
CW	DAF SB120/Wrightbus Cadet 10.2m (Arriva CW1 only).
D	Dennis Dart/Plaxton Pointer 9.8m (First D605 only).
DA	DAF SB220/Optare Delta (Stagecoach).
DA	Dennis Dart SLF/Alexander ALX200 8.9m (Connex).
DA	Dennis Dart SLF/Alexander ALX200 10.2m (Armchair).
DCL	Dennis Dart SLF/Caetano Nimbus 10.7m (Connex, East Thames Buses).
DDL	Dennis Dart SLF/Plaxton Pointer 2 10.1m (Arriva).
DE	Dennis Dart SLF/East Lancs Spryte 10.3m (First).
DHL	Dennis Dart SLF/Caetano Nimbus 10.5m (First).

DL   Dennis Dart SLF/Plaxton Pointer 10.0m or Pointer 2 10.1m (Metroline).

DL   Dennis Dart SLF/Alexander ALX200 10.8m or Plaxton Pointer 2 11.3m (Stagecoach).

DLA   Dennis Lance/Alexander PS (First DLA796 only).

DLD   Dennis Dart SLF/Plaxton Pointer 2 10.1m dual door (Metroline).

DLF   Dennis Dart SLF/Plaxton Pointer 9.2m or 10.0m, or Pointer 2 10.1m (Thorpes).

DLM   Dennis Dart SLF/Plaxton Pointer 2 8.8m (Metroline).

DLS   Dennis Dart SLF/Plaxton Pointer 9.2m (Metroline).

DM   Dennis Dart SLF/Marshall Capital 9.3m (First) or 9.8m (Metroline DM242 only).

DM   Dennis Dart SLF/Alexander ALX200 10.2m or Plaxton Pointer 2 10.1m (Stagecoach).

DML   Dennis Dart SLF/Marshall Capital 10.2m (First, Metroline).

DML   Dennis Dart SLF/Marshall Capital 9.3m (London Central/London General).

DMS   Dennis Dart SLF/Marshall Capital 9.3m (Metroline).

DMS   Dennis Dart SLF/Marshall Capital 8.9m (First, London Central/London General).

DN   Dennis Dart SLF/Caetano Nimbus 11.0m (Blue Triangle).

DNL   Dennis Dart/Northern Counties Paladin 9.0m (Metroline).

DP   Dennis Dart/Plaxton Pointer 9.0m (Arriva, First, Metroline).

DP   Dennis Dart SLF/Plaxton Pointer 2 8.8m (Connex, Armchair DP962 only).

DP   Dennis Dart SLF/Plaxton Pointer 10.0m or Pointer 2 10.1m (Armchair).

DP   Dennis Dart SLF/Plaxton Pointer 2 10.7m (London United).

DPK   Dennis Dart SLF/Plaxton Pointer 2 8.8m (London United).

DPL   Dennis Dart/Plaxton Pointer 9.0m (London Central/London General).

DPL   Dennis Dart SLF/Plaxton Pointer 2 10.7m (Connex).

DPP   Dennis Dart SLF/Plaxton Pointer 10.0m (Arriva).

DPS   Dennis Dart SLF/Plaxton Pointer 2 10.1m (London United).

DR   Dennis Dart/Plaxton Pointer 8.5m (Arriva, London Central/London General, London United, Metroline.)

DR   Dennis Dart/Plaxton Pointer 9.0m (First).

DRL   Dennis Dart/Plaxton Pointer 9.0m (Arriva, London Central, London United, Metroline).

DRN   Dennis Dart/Northern Counties Paladin 9.0m (Arriva).

DS   Dennis Dart SLF/Alexander ALX200 9.4m or Plaxton Pointer 2 9.3m (Stagecoach).

DSD   Dennis Dart SLF/Plaxton Pointer 2 9.2m dual door (Metroline).

DSS   Dennis Dart SLF/Alexander ALX200 8.9m or Plaxton Pointer 2 8.8m (Stagecoach).

DT   Dennis Dart/Duple-Carlyle Dartline 8.5m (London United DT12 only).

DW   Dennis Dart/Wright Handybus 8.5m (First).

DWL   Dennis Dart/Wright Handybus 9.0m (East Thames).

DWL   DAF SB120/Wrightbus Cadet 10.2m or 10.8m (Arriva).

EC   Mercedes-Benz Citaro (First).

EDR   Dennis Dart/Plaxton Pointer 9.8m (Metroline).

ELS   Scania N94UB/East Lancs Myllennium 10.6m (East Thames Buses).

ES   Mercedes-Benz Sprinter (First).

GLS   National Greenway (Blue Triangle).

HDC   Dennis Dart SLF/Caetano Nimbus 10.5m (Hackney Community Transport).

L   Dennis Dart SLF/Plaxton Pointer 10.0m (First).

LCY   Dennis Dart SLF/Alexander ALX200 10.2m (Stagecoach).

LD   Dennis Dart/Plaxton Pointer 9.8m (Epsom).

LDP   Dennis Dart SLF/Plaxton Pointer 9.2m or 10.0m (London Central/London General).

LDP   Dennis Dart SLF/Plaxton Pointer 2 8.8m, 9.3m, 10.1m or 10.7m (London Central/London General).

LDR   Dennis Dart/Plaxton Pointer 9.8m (Arriva).

LLW   Dennis Lance SLF/Wright Pathfinder (First, London United, Metroline).

LS   Leyland National (Thorpes, London United).

MA   Mercedes-Benz Citaro-G articulated bus (Stagecoach)

MAL   Mercedes-Benz Citaro-G articulated bus (London Central/London General).

MB   Mercedes-Benz Vario/Plaxton Beaver (Epsom, Stagecoach).

MBT   Iveco Turbo-Daily 59.12/Marshall (Arriva).

MD   DAF SB220LF/East Lancs Myllennium (London Central).

MM   Mercedes-Benz Vario/Marshall (First).

MM   MAN 11.220/Marshall (Metroline).

MMS   Mercedes-Benz 811D/Marshall (Metroline MMS269 only).

MRL   Optare MetroRider 9.2m (Metroline).

MV   MAN 11.190/Optare Vecta (London United).

OM   Optare MetroRider 8.5m (First, Metroline).

OP   Optare Solo 8.5m (Epsom).

OSL   Optare Solo 8.5m (Thorpes).

PD   Dennis Dart/Plaxton Pointer 9.8m (Stagecoach).

PDL   Dennis Dart SLF/Plaxton Pointer 2 8.8m or 10.7m (Arriva)

S   Optare Solo 8.5m (Connex).

SD   Dennis Dart SLF/Alexander ALX200 8.9m or Plaxton Pointer 2 8.8m (Epsom).

SLD   Dennis Dart SLF/Pointer or ALX200 (Stagecoach).

SLW   Scania N113CRL/Wright Pathfinder (Stagecoach).

VS   Volvo B6BLE/East Lancs Spryte 10.9m (Thorpes).

VWL   Volvo B7L/Wrightbus Eclipse (London Central VWL1 only).

XL   Optare Excel (London United).

FLEET TOTALS at 1st January 2003

The fleet totals are grouped in type order, and cover all types used on TfL services. These totals omit vehicles mentioned in the miscellaneous operations section, so as to give a more accurate picture of vehicles available for mainstream TfL routes. Therefore, contract, training and sightseeing buses are not included here. Types are grouped in matching order of chassis/body manufacturers. Variations of body styling of the same manufacturer, length or door arrangements are ignored for the purposes of these tables.

Routemasters (629)
AEC Routemaster/Park Royal (629)

Step-entrance double-deckers (1108)
DAF DB250/Northern Counties (2)
Dennis Arrow/East Lancs (35)
Dennis Arrow/Northern Counties (6)
Leyland Olympian/Alexander (40)
Leyland Olympian/ECW (156)
Leyland Olympian/Leyland (3)
Leyland Olympian/Northern Counties (65)
Leyland Titan (18)
MCW Metrobus (195)
Scania N113DRB/Alexander (10)
Volvo B10M Citybus/Alexander (38)
Volvo B10M Citybus/East Lancs (13)
Volvo Olympian/Alexander (162)
Volvo Olympian/East Lancs (57)
Volvo Olympian/Northern Counties (308)

Low-floor double-deckers (2928)
DAF DB250LF/Alexander ALX400 (346)
DAF DB250LF/Optare Spectra (6)
DAF DB250LF/Plaxton President (101)
Dennis Trident/Alexander ALX400 (953)
Dennis Trident/East Lancs Lolyne (51)
Dennis Trident/Plaxton President (547)
Volvo B7TL/Alexander ALX400 (110)
Volvo B7TL/East Lancs Vyking (53)
Volvo B7TL/Plaxton President (559)
Volvo B7TL/Wrightbus Eclipse Gemini (202)

Step-entrance single-deck buses (283)
Dennis Dart/Northern Counties Paladin (36)
Dennis Dart/Plaxton Pointer (161)
Dennis Dart/Wright Handybus (11)
Dennis Lance/Alexander PS (1)
Leyland Lynx (3)
MAN 11.220/Marshall (20)
Mercedes-Benz 709D/711D/811D (11)
Mercedes-Benz Vario (31)
Optare MetroRider (9)

Low-floor single-deck buses (2743)
DAF SB120/Wrightbus Cadet (70)
DAF SB220LF/East Lancs Myllennium (17)
Dennis Dart SLF/Alexander ALX200 (308)
Dennis Dart SLF/Caetano Compass (14)
Dennis Dart SLF/Caetano Nimbus (82)
Dennis Dart SLF/East Lancs Spryte (20)
Dennis Dart SLF/Marshall Capital (576)
Dennis Dart SLF/Plaxton Pointer (1418)
Dennis Dart SLF/Wright Crusader (8)
Dennis Lance SLF/Wright Pathfinder (24)
Fiat Ducato (4)
Mercedes-Benz Citaro (11)
Mercedes-Benz Citaro-G (35)
Mercedes-Benz Sprinter (3)
Optare Excel (29)
Optare Solo (59)
Scania N94UB/East Lancs Myllennium (14)
Scania N113CRL/Wright Pathfinder (16)
Scania OmniCity (1)
Volvo B6BLE/East Lancs Spryte (23)
Volvo B6BLE/Wrightbus Crusader (3)
Volvo B7L/Wrightbus Eclipse (1)
Volvo B10BLE/Alexander ALX300 (7)